Contents

Archie and his
mum are going
to a café.

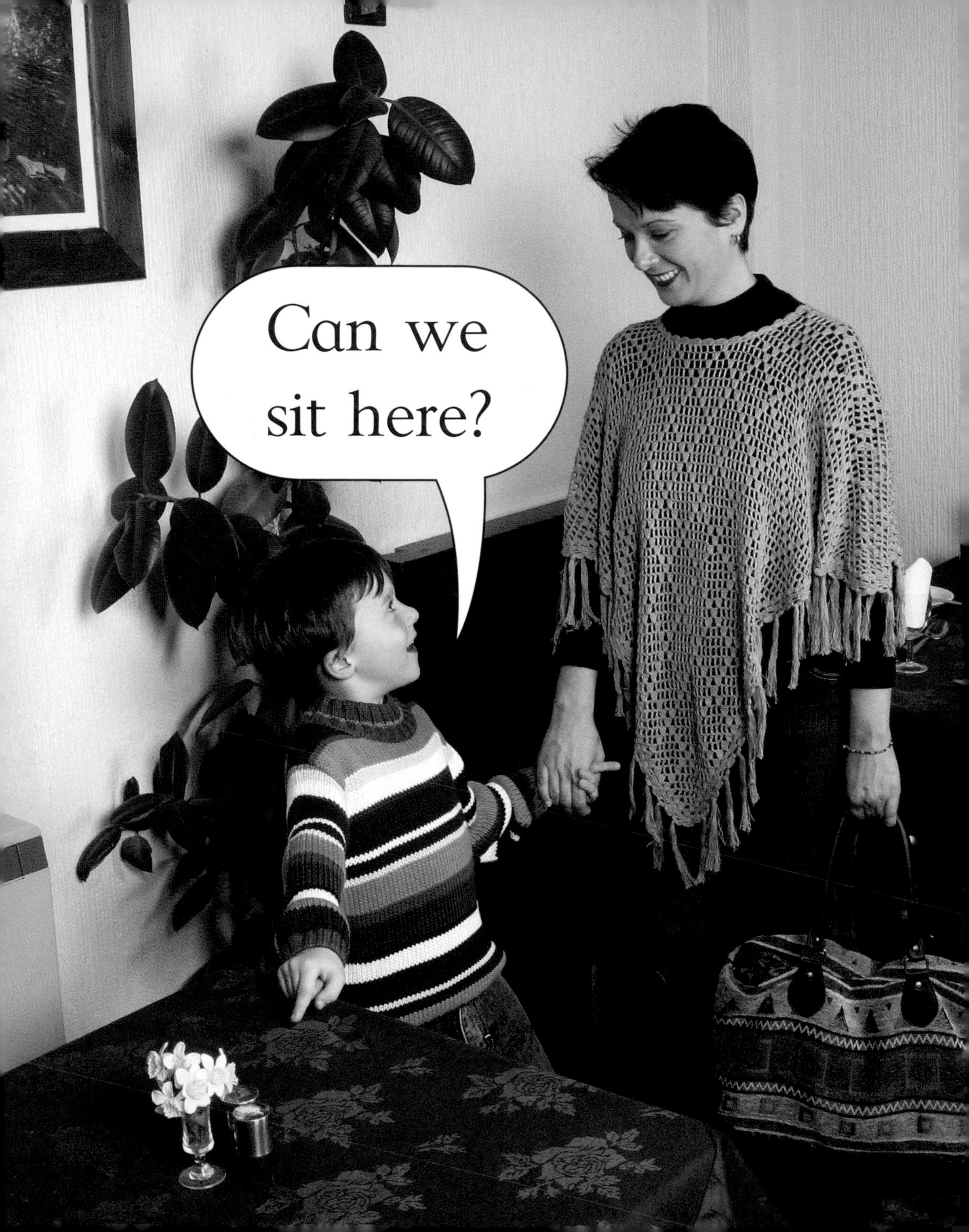
Can we sit here?

7

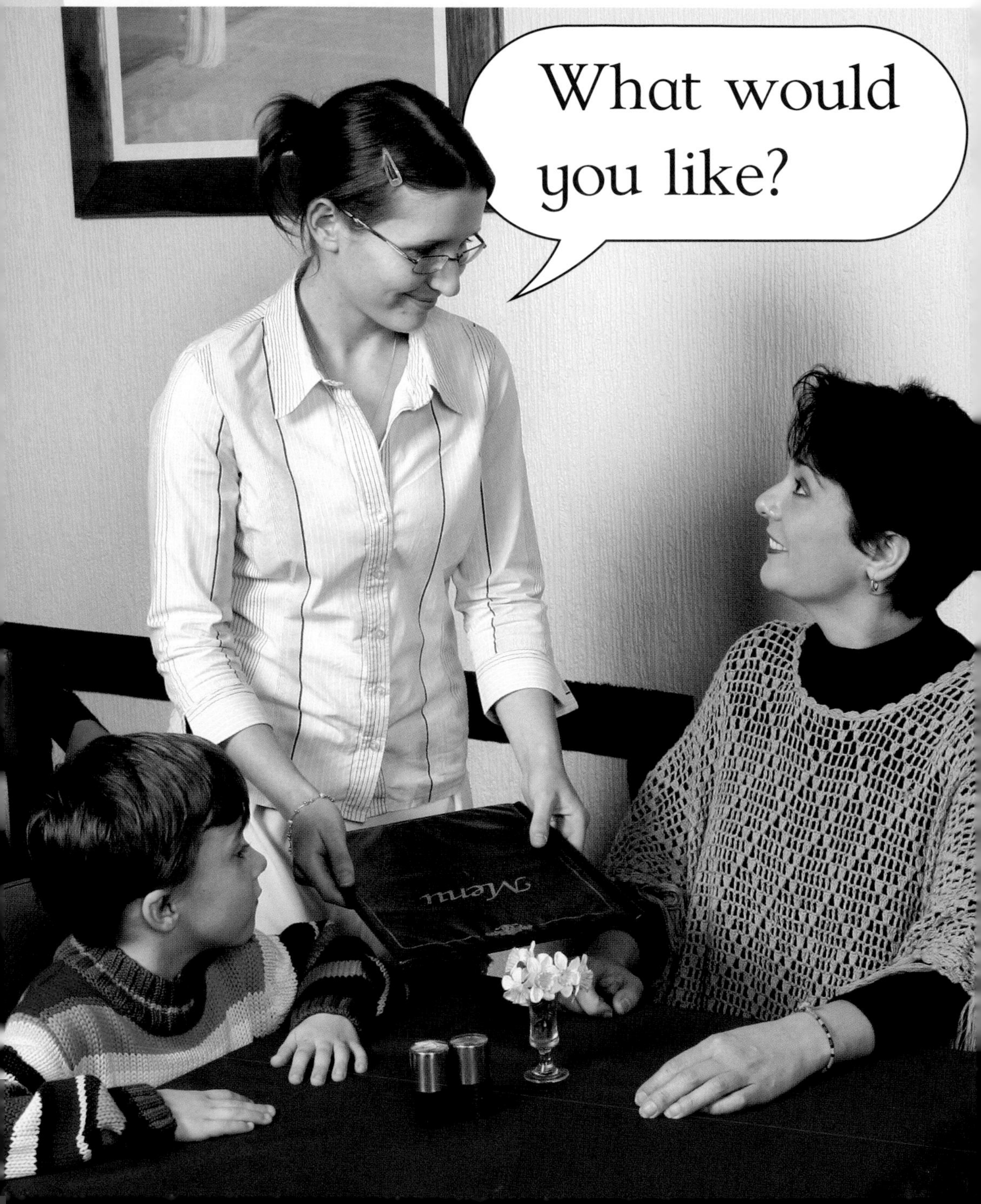
What would you like?
Menu

MENU

Drinks

Tea..
Coffee.. 80p
Hot Chocolate.. £1.00
Fruit Juice (apple, orange, pineapple) £1.50
Milkshake.. 95p
Milk.. £1.10
Mineral Water.. 90p

Cakes

Toasted Tea Cake...................................... £1.00
Scone with butter ....
Scone with jam and cream............... 95p
Gingerbread Man........................... 90p
Danish Pastry................................. £1.10
£1.00
£1.10

10

And I'd like a coffee, please.

First the waitress chooses a gingerbread man.

13

Then she pours the coffee.

She takes the tray to Archie and his mum.

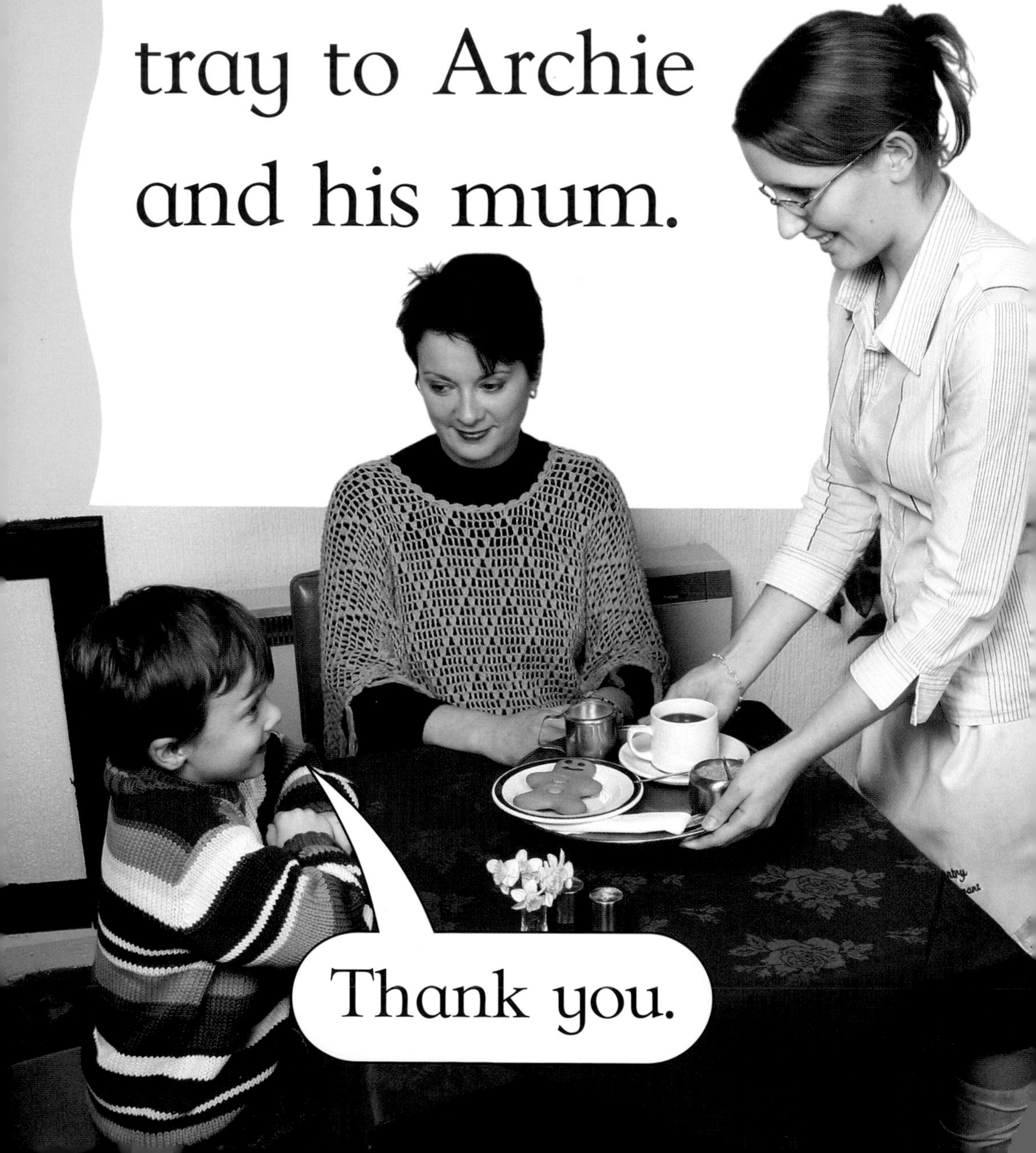

Archie takes
a bite of his
gingerbread
man.

19

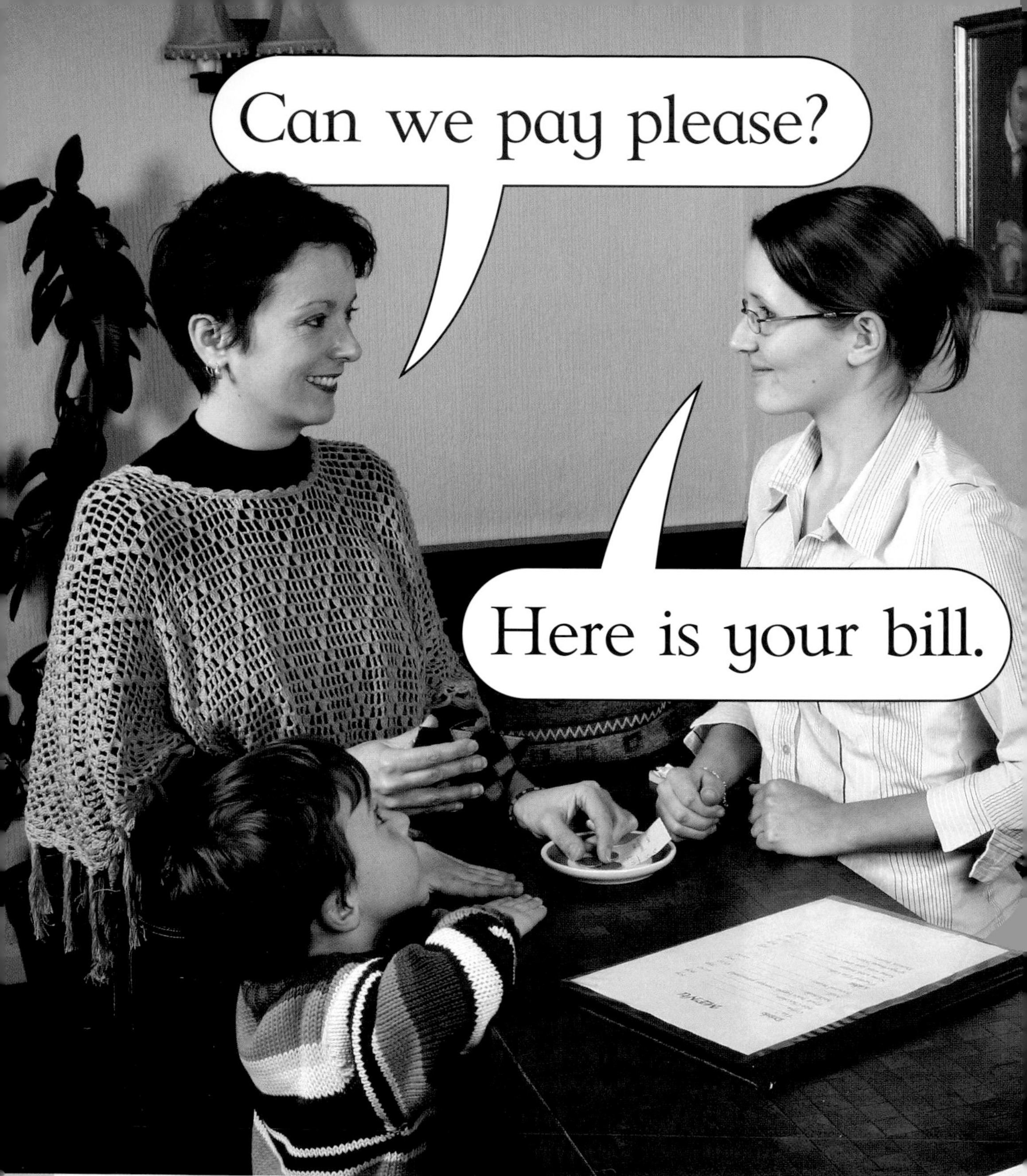
Can we pay please?
Here is your bill.

21

23

Word bank

Look back for these words and pictures.

Bill

Café

Coffee

Gingerbread man

Menu

Pay

Pours

Tray

Waitress